Hi! I'm Joe.
I have a special story to tell you.
Part of it is about me.
And part of it is about you!

Did you know that God
  loves all people?
God loves me.
God loves _____.
(child's name)

God sent His Son Jesus to die
  on the cross for all people.
God takes care of me.
God takes care of

_____.
(child's name)

He gives us the things we need.

God wants me to stay healthy.
He gives me food to eat.
I really like pizza!

God blesses _____ with food, too.
(child's name)

_____ likes to eat _____.
(child's name)                                (food)

God wants me to stay warm.
He gives me clothes to wear.
I really like my five-pocket jeans!

God blesses _____ with clothes, too.
(child's name)

_____ likes to wear _____.
(child's name)                              (clothing)

God helps me stay strong.
He lets me exercise and play.
I really like swimming.

God helps _____ to do things, too.
(child's name)

_____ likes to _____ .
(child's name)                    (activity)

God wants me to take care of the body He gave me.

I wash every day.
Sometimes I make a beard with soap bubbles!

God gave _____ a wonderful body, too.
(child's name)

Take good care of it.

God gives us sleep so our bodies can rest.
I go to bed when my parents say.
God watches over me while I sleep.
God watches over _____ , too.
(child's name)

I love God. He first loved me.
He takes care of my every need.

I thank Him every day for His goodness.

God cares for you, too,

_____.
(child's name)

Here is a prayer you can speak to the Lord.
Thank You, Lord, for taking care
Of me each night and day.
I know that you are with me,
At work, at rest, at play. Amen.